M000041622

ARIEL SIMMONDS

Quint*essential*

The *Essential* Master Guide
to Achieving Your Fullest Self

Quintessential

Quint*essential*

ISBN: 978-0-578-48934-6 (Paperback)
ISBN: 978-0-578-48935-3 (eBook)

Front cover image by Gregory Wright
Book cover design by Ariel Simmonds and Gregory Wright

Printed by Ingram Content Group, in the United States of America

First printing edition 2019

Ariel Simmonds
A Novel Idea
Morganville, NJ 07751
www.novelideaa.com

It doesn't take anything
away from **you** to

share knowledge.

People can only

do with it what **they** are

capable of doing
with it.

– Sonia Simmonds

PROLOGUE

Quintessential is more than just a book to me. It's a mantra, a movement, and the messages in this book are aspirational.

I never dreamt of writing a book. It was only when I was exhausted by the imperceptibility of my purpose that I brought my thoughts together, listened to my own advice, drew on my years of education, and set out to aid myself and others in finding and fulfilling their inner purpose.

When you manifest your fullest being, the external joys of life will flow into you in ways beyond your imagination. I felt something in myself that I needed to share with other women and girls, with my future children, with those around me, and ultimately with myself.

Enjoy my first book.

~Ariel Simmonds

CONTENTS

Quintessential

1 | TAKE TWO

Since the nineties, I have always fantasized the seasons of the year just the way they were taught, and I expect I'll do the same into my nineties. When I think of summer, I imagine myself eating rosy-pink, strawberry ice cream on top of a crisp waffle cone as I walk along the sidewalks of the suburbs. I remember sweating in the heat of June at my desk in elementary school, or in the house when the air conditioning was broken. I can also recall gazing out the window, observing the dreamlike baby-blue water confined to my family's inground pool.

In the fall, I envision brown, purple, and faintly red leaves floating gracefully to a bed of dead remnants below what was once a beautifully shady tree. I can channel the sense of deceleration that comes with the transition to winter, when the possibilities of adventure and exploration that lay in the front yard would abate for months to come.

During the winter, snow, of course. I see inches upon inches of a white blanket hiding the grass on the lawn. And I see a long red shovel leaning against the garage, the only color in sight.

With spring, I think of more than just memories or fantasies. On a rudimentary level, I picture springtime as painted with cerulean skies, exuberant pink, red, and yellow flowers, freshly sheared grass, and beautiful butterflies fluttering amid the buzzing bees. I long to inhale the scent of the rain on the warm concrete, to hear the jingle of the first ice cream truck serenading the streets, and to say goodbye to my winter coats until the brisk fall returns. Though this particular fantasy is usually trumped by an extension of winter, halting the advancement of nature's beauty and the other perks that the season brings, I am always hopeful for this transformative time of year.

Spring is a metamorphic time when the weather turns more favorable, seasonal discomfort and depression elude, and our individual worlds are born again. Spring resembles hope: another day, another opportunity—much like the opportunity you have today to redesign the strongest, fiercest version of yourself.

We've all heard the dictum that you can't choose your family but you can choose your friends. Well, you can't choose your race either, but you can choose whether you'll permit the clichés that are affixed to it to define you. You can't choose the economic class you're born into, but you can choose whether you'll redefine who you may have assumed you were inclined to become and whether you will be the root of generational wealth and success in your family. And you can't choose the sex you're born into, but if you turn out to be a woman—well, you're blessed.

What is the world without women? We create, we resolve, we build, we elevate, we lead, we advocate, we comfort, and we love. Need I say more? We are not only the future, we are right now.

Women today are shaping the way we understand our communities, our country, and our world cognizant that life is for living, and opportunities are for taking. In every corner of the media, women of all ages, races, sexualities, and cultures are embodying a renewed fierceness and independence. The voice of women has been amplified, our drive has permeated culture, and our resilience is sustained and undying.

These instances of abundantly powerful women are not a coincidence. Women of the world, now more than ever, are defining their lives by their own means and with their own ideas of success. Success isn't something that just happens for some people. It arises from the intentional attainment of well-defined goals that eventually amount to accomplishments.

◆◆◆

I was raised not to show up empty-handed. This could be observed in the simplest of actions: at a young age it meant bringing my own toothpaste when sleeping out, bringing my own towel to a friend's pool, or kindly asking if anything else was needed before arriving at a function (fingers crossed that the answer would be no, because who really wants it to be yes?).

Through adolescence and adulthood, this concept led me to always be prepared with a resumé reserved in my email for spontaneous networking. I would also keep an auxiliary cache of money on hold for emergencies. Equally important, I'd always have an extra piece of gum in my pocket or bag. This was mainly the result of knowing that everyone would ask for *just one piece* upon discovering my stash.

The underlying message was to stay prepared. I was taught that this was paramount, therefore, I wouldn't waste valuable time or miss an opportunity while scrambling to get myself or my supplements in order. You never know when it will be your time to shine. You never know when your life will change completely for the better. Being prepared when it's your time to go is the best start to success. This preparation gives you leverage over your decisions when opportunity comes knocking.

Successful women today use the same principle of leverage to surpass their wildest expectations by staying ready to snatch the opportunity as it comes into reach. The best way to advance in life is to put yourself in a position where you're worthy and capable of advancement.

Despite the remarkableness of women and our increased visibility and excellence, we shouldn't forget that we are not too far removed from the days when women didn't have equal rights or equal opportunities. I remember my sixth-grade teacher schooling us on the challenges faced by women and African Americans before the passage of the fifteenth and nineteenth amendments. (In a brief American history lesson, I'll remind you that the fifteenth amendment to the U.S. Constitution prohibits the denial of voting on the basis of race or color, and the nineteenth prohibits the same on the basis of gender.) After elaborating on the hurdles put in place to prevent women and black people from voting, my teacher said words that implanted themselves in my memory: *Imagine being black and being a woman at the same time! Jeez!*

Fast forward to today, about a century after both of those laws had been enacted, I still say *Jeez* when thinking about the obstacles and unfairness between women and men, and between blacks and whites.

Pressing beyond subtly unsubtle barriers and the deliberate exclusion of women from various spaces of life, living today and knowing that women have projected their way into the rooms they've been shut out of and participated in conversations they weren't asked to be part of is remarkable. Decades of observing women's history and the application of leverage through the triumphs of womanhood have inculcated tactics for advancement into the minds of women today. These lessons of preparation and in being quick to snatch opportunities should be your own ignition to a successful life.

Expect to succeed but get there intentionally. Prepare yourself, set out to do something, and make sure you actually do it. You are more than capable of conquering your vision of success, but the only way you'll get there is by understanding one of life's key truths: You have to live and lead with purpose. Life will be boring, unclear, and frustrating if you live with no sense of direction, let alone the desire to get anywhere. Only when you are confident of your worth, your destiny, and your why, will you truly know yourself and feel at peace.

You set the standard for how others will treat, view, and respect you. When you lack intentions or direction in your life, you are subject to missed opportunities and bad relationships. For instance, if you lack confidence in the workplace, you're less likely to get the project or deal that will boost your professional life. Likewise in your love life, if you don't respect and love yourself, others will not be inclined to hold you to a higher standard. Without a distinct understanding of your purpose at work or your intentions in a relationship, you cannot expect to reap greatness from either. The balance in your life is rational, and thankfully, it can be altered to the positive, as it's all within your control.

No matter where you are in life, single, dating, married, or somewhere in between, it's never too late to get closer to your purpose. By living intentionally, you can achieve personal success, uncompromisable happiness, and a healthy relationship with yourself and others. The key to a full and successful life is something you'll find once you are cognizant of who you truly are and take the responsibility of prioritizing yourself. By shifting your focus to mastering, fulfilling, and concentrating on yourself, you will reap bountiful dividends in success—personally, socially, and occupationally.

However, preserving a strong focus is not always easy. It's important to maintain a deep focus not just on your goals, but on yourself overall. You have to be aware of where your focus is directed and where your mind roams. When we lose concentration on ourselves—or worse, when we put a higher value on others than on ourselves—a great barrier arises between ourselves and our goals. For instance, putting more energy into being in a relationship than into living your best, most purposeful life is a bit of an anomaly. The fruit you reap from self-understanding and fulfillment will be the most confident and most sensible you, and this version of you will attract and sustain the most genuine relationships with others.

Relationships require patience, understanding, and love. Love whomever you choose, wherever and whenever you choose. Acknowledge where your focus is directed and where your mind roams, but don't allow others to project your life or assume your limitations. The one imposition I will make is that I hope deeply that you require the same patience, understanding, and love of yourself first.

Seek to understand yourself before trying to understand others. I don't say this to undermine the importance of understanding the people around you, but you will nurture better relationships if you first understand yourself.

Self-reflection is where you must begin. Understand who you are and why you are this person. Don't just speak; know what you are saying, know from where it developed, and why you say it. Encompass what's important to you and seek a concrete explanation of why you value it. Knowing who you are and following your purpose through your daily strides is a great way to fulfill yourself and receive your greatest blessings. These blessings include financial success, unconditional and lasting love, and most importantly loving yourself for who you really are.

All these things can be mastered *at the same time* when you fulfill and prioritize yourself. Minimize the energy you put into seeking out others, and maximize your eagerness to find yourself. People will be enthralled by you, by your drive, and by your confidence. By any measure, focus on developing into your best, and the best will follow.

One common trouble that can shake the bridge that connects us to our greatest accomplishments is social pressure about when you "should" be married or dating. A frequent buffer to conversation, especially among families, is the question of whether you're in a relationship yet. Though this is not the most abrasive pressure to put on someone, it can ring frustration, confusion, and urgency in one's head that is entirely fictitious.

Women are expected to be married by a certain age. We are expected to be pregnant by a certain age. Wouldn't it be a powerful twist to shift the expectations of women from the personal to the professional? What if the question went from whether you are in a relationship yet to whether you have plans to *own a business yet?* I think developing our greatest selves is very important because this version of ourselves will go a long way towards setting the foundations to a great relationship and family.

Women play a vital role in human reproduction, obviously. We can't ignore the fact that our biological clocks tick louder than mechanical clocks in a classroom full of test takers, and the pressure to find a spouse can be hard to escape, especially as a woman grows older. But family, and even society, poking at you when it's supposedly time for you to enter "womanhood" can trigger an internal pressure and distraction resulting in stress.

You may also feel divisions within yourself. You may feel that there's no optimal truce between *Yeah, they're right* and *My time is coming, I'm good.* This can ignite self-doubt, feelings of insufficiency, and anger toward yourself within yourself. Before long, you may start comparing yourself to others. It may suddenly resonate with you that the girl you went to middle school with is engaged, and that your cousin who's a year younger than you is pregnant. Swiftly now, you feel that you're not pretty enough or fun enough, and that you're losing the race.

To make matters worse, you may already have noticed how many millennials fall hopelessly into a black hole of resistance when it comes to relationship commitment. I can recall archives of this dating back to middle school, when people stopped dating and coined the term "talking" to mean something less than a relationship. Yeah, I'm confused too.

In any situation, take this as a note to yourself: *There is no competition.* When you stop worrying about others more than you worry about yourself, you'll come to terms with this. It will then resonate with you that you are on time in your life, and you will reap the happiness that comes with living in the present. Stay in the present. It's where your body is and where your life is. Have your mind meet you there as well. Your *now* is the only realm of your life that you can edit and control. Get yourself out of this imaginative competition and start loving who you are and where you are today.

The idea of competition can easily be mistaken for comparison or insecurity. Neither of those is a winning quality. Comparison is just another barrier to success. Once you acknowledge this, you can conquer it.

Insecurities are often more frequent and overbearing during the dark times of our lives. Insecurities have a way of restricting us from achieving our fullest potential. But critical thinking offers us an alternative way to deal with self-doubt. Acknowledging your hesitancy and lack of confidence is the perfect place to start.

Times of unexpected and frazzled diffidence

are the best moments to use critique and brainstorm the best solution to an impending problem. Think before acting. Don't do because of others. Act out of confidence, not comparison.

In life, we are expected to perform. *Work harder, study more, get this done, make sure that gets handled.* It's in these areas that we want to excel and elevate ourselves for our own good or for the benefit of society at large. Let this be your competition—but not against *her* or *him*. Just against who you were yesterday.

Seeking advice and guidance on your journey through life can be very helpful. However, I find that when you listen to other people too heavily, you taint your own judgement and start to doubt your thoughts as a result of their differing opinions. Gain insight and wisdom, but also trust yourself and be confident in your ideas.

Possess a clear understanding of your values, desires, and priorities. Get in tune with your mind, body, and soul. Often, the foundation you need to motivate yourself through uncertainty is built on your confidence in what you want and knowing how badly you want it. Never lose sight of your goals and who you want to be.

A concrete understanding of yourself will be necessary when you are combatting supposed gender roles. The media can consciously or unconsciously influence and shape our perspective on what it means to be a woman or to be a man. Social constructs are mistaken for uncompromisable law, especially in relation to women. The socially constructed roles that make up our complex identities hold great accountability for the ways in which we perceive ourselves. These standards can place expectations on women and may lead some to feel that they must comply. Even more importantly, the perceptions through which children understand the world will lead to them growing up with an utterly false narrative that assumes conformity.

There are some top-level careers and roles that still lack any representation by women. Because men have a long history in these positions, such roles may be associated with their gender. We need to level the playing field and illustrate to young people and society that this does not have to be the case.

Throughout his adolescence, my brother was encouraged to become an engineer. Only a baffling 11% of practicing engineers are women, and only 9% are in leadership roles. With these statistics, it's no surprise that I was unaware of what an engineer was until college. The details of engineering careers along with their financial promises and prestige, were conveyed to my male counterpart but not to me.

All of this is to say that we have to find a way to overcome the commonplace frustrations, distractions, and inequality that are served to women. This can start when we gain confidence, understand ourselves, and inch toward our purpose day after day.

What do you want out of your life? Some days when I wake up, I'm eager, ready to take on the world and be the best at what I do. Other days, I feel unmotivated, stuck, and distant from my own self. But when I ask myself what I want out of life, I have a few things in mind.

I want a family of my own with children who fill the open space with laughter. I want a husband and deep love, and I want really great friends. I want a house that is a home. I want to travel and touch every continent. I want to work in a career that I love until I run my own businesses. I want residual income flowing into my bank account as I sleep. I want to be admired and remembered as a woman with strong qualities.

These arbitrary-seeming wishes aren't random. All of these are things that I deem as peaceful. They are what make me giddy inside. Above all else, I want happiness in my life.

I am happy at present, but I'm a work in progress seeking personal fulfillment. This is an ongoing, interminable journey, but one with plenty of successes that makes the voyage worthwhile. The journey is what makes me happy.

Success will be defined differently by everyone you ask. I don't think material items, a million dollars, property, or cars make you successful. I think that success is mastering yourself, in three different respects or views. Let's work our way up to the most important one.

View number three is your ability to balance yourself when you are paired with others, in relationships, friendships, or elsewhere. Ask yourself:

Do I minimize who I am to accommodate others?

_____

Do I set a higher priority on spending time with others than on spending time with myself?

_____

Do I feel mentally stimulated by the people I surround myself with?

_____

Jot down your answers. In chapter four, I'll expand

on this concept.

View number two involves how you manage your inner being. You can't expect success if you are not first in touch with your mind, body, and soul. Ask yourself:

> There are twenty-four hours in a day. How much of that time do I devote to my personal, physical, and mental health?

> _____

> How deeply do I understand my motives, thoughts, and emotions?

> _____

> Am I capable of admitting when I need help?

> _____

Record your thoughts. In chapter three, I'll deliver gems about how to start understanding your mental capacities and shortcomings.

The third and most pressing view of yourself is about being or becoming your own woman. This is important because being your own person without living by the standards of others will offer you the release that you need for inner peace, success, and genuine fulfilment. Ask yourself:

How confident am I in myself and in my future?

_____

What goals have I set for the next year, and what accomplishments have I achieved recently?

_____

How substantially do I prioritize myself in my life?

_____

We often forget that we must prioritize ourselves over everyone else. Is this selfish? Unreasonable? If you're not your best or at least trying to be, how can you expect to be an asset or a helping hand to others? What credibility would you possess? In chapter two, I'll explain this comprehensively.

Again, success is not measured by the dollar, the

assets, the fame, or the popularity. These things, ideas, and acknowledgements will satisfy your materialistic cravings, financial goals, and pending obligations. But you need to realize that you are not alive just to pay bills, get by, and fill your lungs with great deep breaths every morning while rolling your eyes at your alarm clock at the crack of dawn.

True happiness comes with pure happiness. Finding supreme confidence in who you are, mastering personal satisfaction within yourself, and having friends and relationships who raise you up are what I find to be the characteristics of true success. The key is to master your own life.

Happiness yields more happiness. When you give off good energy, you will receive it in return. And if I'm wrong, you'll still be so joyous that you won't be fazed by anyone else's negativity.

Like anything else in life, success doesn't come easily. It doesn't come from an occasional grind, it comes from a consistent one. You must seek your fullest self, know her, and then become her fearlessly. You have to look beyond your worries about risk and failure. Alternatively, you must train yourself to see your shortcomings as lessons, not failures at all. Eliminate any thoughts that cast doubt on your greatness or minimize your excitement about winning.

Becoming a woman of such high stature and

confidence is a power that surges beyond you. It will shift your life. It's powerful because it's personal. Get to know yourself deeply. The return on a genuine understanding of yourself and satisfaction in who you are is immeasurable. You'll become better, stronger, smarter, and bolder.

The opportunities that women of today have snatched were not so accessible years ago. To continue the upward mobility of women in our society, we need to be the change so that we can teach the change to those who are crawling beside us. We need to expound on the importance of personal fulfillment, focus, and elevation, because those are the makings of true eternal success.

Despite the way we saw life depicted in princess movies when we were little girls, your life may not be a fairytale. But I promise you that it can be a success story. Within this book lies the secrets, the master file, the ultimate guide to mastering, fulfilling, and prioritizing yourself, which will make you the ideal recipient for a full, promising, beautiful life. You have many successes to come in your future, and I want you to live a full life.

You will find love and all the supplementary joys of life, but you will find them more readily once you know yourself. A happy and successful life is attainable, and it begins with the choice to live your life for yourself, in the way you choose. I don't know if you realize how amazing you are, can be, and will be.

It's never too late or too early to start investing in your best life, your most freeing life—a balanced life, defined by your version of success. Happiness starts with embracing and becoming your own woman, growing into your fullest self (mind, body, and soul), and conquering the balance of relationships and your personal destiny.

I believe that this is the only life I will ever live. This may be the only life you will ever live too, so let's get it right.

In these pages, together we'll conquer becoming our own uniquely independent selves, we'll access the keys to personal fulfillment, and we'll balance our personal fates with our external relationships. Together, we will explore and apprehend the quint*essential* opportunity to evolve into becoming a fierce, empowered, reborn, boss woman.

BE THE LEADER OF YOUR LIFE

What are some of your most defining characteristics?

_____

_____

_____

Where do you want to be by the end of the year?

_____

_____

_____

Where do you want to be in five years? Ten years?

_____

_____

_____

Why do you want this? *Why **must** you achieve your goals?*

_____

_____

_____

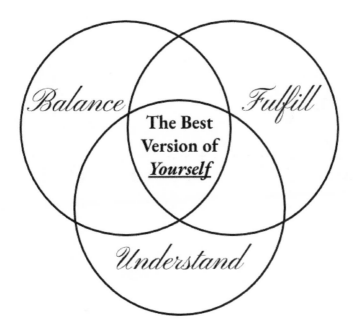

2 | RESURGENCE

Is a dog crate a prison for punishments or a sanctuary for a pet's personal escape?

We got my dog when I was eleven. Her crate was her designated area to go to when no one was around to supervise her and where she was sent as punishment for misbehaving. I'm not sure exactly when she began to think of it as a space for taking naps, hiding stolen socks, and retreating to eat bacon-flavored treats in exclusivity. I guess life is all about perspective, and maybe it's even about refusing to be a prisoner in your own life by recognizing the true power within yourself.

It is only a disservice to yourself to see life as an imprisonment. Though not all circumstances can be resolved or leveled so easily, your perspective and actions can be pivotal in reconstructing your life.

Getting from Point A to Point B is never as simple as a smooth ride down one long road. There are stops, turns, yields, and sometimes complete detours. Similarly, when we create intentions in our lives, even with detailed directions, we shouldn't be taken aback when we don't arrive by the paved path we'd planned on. We aren't perfect predictors of the future.

Life happens, and the unexpected should be expected. Achieving your greatest successes and conquering yourself isn't something you'd stumble upon at the end of a simple straight road. Anticipate trials, tribulations, errors, and breaks, but be optimistic in knowing that even though creating a full life is no easy task, it will be worth it.

Throughout my life I have come across and shortly after adhered to certain principles that are universal, uncomplicated, and applicable to all facets of life. We'll visit them throughout this chapter.

Explaining to someone of an older generation that it's possible to succeed without following the traditional path of becoming a doctor, lawyer, or engineer is difficult in its own right because it requires you to believe it's possible too. Both your family and the world acknowledge that these careers are promising and fulfilling, and most people feel confident that they will afford you the opportunity to live an opulent life. These people are right, and there's proof. But seeking financial success along a less traveled road, especially in an era of vast technological advancements is also an option.

Not everyone fully grasps the immense range of opportunities for people who grew up in this era of technological growth. Maturing alongside technological developments has inspired people to create great avenues for new career ideas, ways to more readily earn passive, active, and portfolio income, and has opened the opportunity to bind your ideas to a global platform. Some of these newly recognized professions have nothing to do with technology itself. Simply knowing how to use technology has given people the potential to uncover new profitable directions in life that are geared toward their personal interests.

Do you remember your answer to the timeless inquiry, *What do you want to be when you get older?* My answer changed from teacher to flight attendant to psychologist to pharmacist to lawyer. This array of professions was probably justified for my nine-year-old self. I remember how my responses always made adults' eyes widen. They were impressed, and I liked the feeling that their excitement and encouragement gave me. I liked doing well in school and hearing how proud my parents were of me. I was confident in their confidence in me. I thrived on other people being proud of me. For a while, this was my primary motivation. At times, I'm still energized by this kind of praise, but all it ultimately has done is intensify my anxiety and stress.

As a kid, when adults glorified me for my choices and thoughts, I was filled with satisfaction. I felt victorious knowing that others were happy, proud, and excited for me. Now, when I catch myself relying on validation, approval, or cheers from others, it invokes pressure. Keeping everyone happy is a heavy burden, mostly because it's impossible. When you lose focus of what makes you happy, life itself becomes a heavy responsibility. Realizing that I should be working hard and making decisions for my own sake, my own pride, and my own happiness made me ponder who I even was, what I wanted, and where I truly wanted to be.

In becoming your own woman and setting yourself up for success, you'll find it necessary to align yourself with three core principles: put yourself first, have goals, and be confident. In rising to your fullest potential, you'll learn that the power to make yourself feel purposeful and happy is all yours. Living just to bring the expectations of others to fruition will never satisfy you because you won't be in control of yourself. The satisfaction will always be for them.

Put yourself first in your life. Take a moment to recognize something that isn't said often enough: Your life is and always has been about you and for you. You are in school to advance your education. You are working to save money to afford your future. You are traveling so you can see the world for yourself and gain a global perspective. This life was created for you, and there is no shame or selfishness in embodying that.

The harsh truth to reconcile with, especially as you get older, is that no one is more invested in you than yourself. This knowledge comes with increased responsibility for yourself. As you develop into yourself and envision large and refreshing ideas, goals, and dreams, you will realize that everything you seek in life will only be achieved if you invest the time. You have to make the calls, do the work, and show up. No one can do this for you.

Just as you need to prioritize yourself, you have to anticipate that others will prioritize themselves too. Despite the undying love your circle may have for you, if they are to love you they must prioritize themselves at some point. And you should encourage them to. They may even have come to a crossroads and acknowledged that they can't help you without first helping themselves. There's nothing wrong with this. In fact, everything is right about it, and you should adhere to this as well.

You are an interminable investment. You know your value, so invest in what you know. Make your life worth your while. Don't wait for a success story, create one. There is no moment more perfect than the present one to change your life for the better. Seize the day, seize your opportunities.

Your responsibility and duty to yourself should be your top priority, which is why you have to refuse the guilt you might feel when prioritizing yourself. There will always be obligations, people who need you, and items of priority. But if you always put off your goals in the expectation that one day all the clutter in your life will clear up, you may be waiting a lifetime. Life is unpredictable and it changes every day. Recognize that the missing factor to a full life is having yourself at the center of it.

I think that practicing a healthy amount of positive selfishness is imperative. Do something solely out of your own interest every once in a while. Even if it's for less than an hour a day, you should periodically check in with yourself to ensure that you're feeling all right. When you neglect yourself, your mood may shift, and you may treat others accordingly.

Moments of positive selfishness are essential. You can't be of great help or be your best self unless you are first fulfilled. It's in these moments that we progress, re-center ourselves, and jolt forward with our best energy, thoughts, and ideas.

What will make you your fiercest self is found not only in what you set out to do, but it is found in your knowledge and plans of how to get it done. It's one thing to have goals, but formulating a plan to reach them is where the real work comes in. We can talk about what we want to do today, but tomorrow we have to make sure that our words evolve into actions. Success comes when opportunity is adjoined to preparation. When you fail to prepare, opportunities will pass you by.

A big dream has much more to it than meets the eye. Stop assuming *This will be my year* and start ensuring that it becomes true. Only then will you be satisfied, successful, and not weeping *Next year will be better* due to missed opportunities. Experiencing your potential and witnessing your grind will make all the reasons for your past shortcomings very clear. Maybe all along, you weren't realizing your full potential.

Your greatest achievements will require you to conquer the smaller goals within your prized goal. Long-term goals are reached by incrementally assembling the pieces of your dream today. This will bring you closer to your main target tomorrow. When you use today to plan and develop, you will get to tomorrow sooner and begin reaping the benefits.

For instance, if you want to lose a lot of weight, be practical. Make a schedule for the gym, build a solid meal plan, and break your goal down by how much you can pragmatically expect to lose in a week, and then a month. Be specific and set measurable goals. Do you want to just lose some weight, or do you want to lose twenty pounds? Measure it out, be consistent, revisit your goals often, and repeat.

Figure out what you want, outline how you will get there, and work on it every day. Incorporate this routine into your daily life. Wake up, brush your teeth, wipe the crust out of your eyes, and get to work. When you have an objective and a destination, all that's left to do is get there.

To blossom into your own woman, consistency is vital. Note that consistency and repetition are not the same thing. Consistency is coming home every day and having chicken on Monday, sushi on Tuesday, steak and potatoes on Wednesday, and maybe sleep for dinner on Thursday because you were too tired to cook. Repetition is having a burger every night. It might not taste bad, but it can get boring, and at some point you have to give yourself a break.

Consistency isn't dull because once you start seeing improvements, you will realize that your dedication was worthwhile, progressive, and even more is achievable. You will also be able to diversify the tasks you take on every day. As long as you're moving toward your goal, you're on the right track. Being consistent will elevate you in your field and bring you closer to your goals. Whether it takes days, weeks, months, or years, progress depends on consistency, including reasonable breaks (hence sleeping for dinner here and there).

If you're consistent, then one day your present will be the future you always dreamed of. Envision how that future will feel. You might feel accomplished, proud, blessed, and maybe even eager to apply your newfound discipline to another task on your to-accomplish list.

Think of yourself as a business. For instance, if your aim is to become well-respected and abundantly profitable in the tech industry, does it make more sense to be consumed with all the latest products and consequently neglecting consumer feedback and satisfaction with existing items? Or would you expect to achieve greater success by focusing on a single technological product or line, thereby ensuring the highest-quality materials, services, and consumer experience, then using this data to progress?

When you focus on only a few of the most important things at a time, you will pay closer attention to detail, anticipate optimal outcomes, and raise your likelihood of success. Sometimes less is more. When you raise too many things to the same level of importance, you subdue the importance of everything else because they all level out and neutralize. Lock in on just a few of your most important goals and take it from there. Not everything that is important is urgent, and not all urgent things are important. Simply put, when everything is important, nothing is.

Pure focus can be misunderstood and seen as standoffish, anal behavior. Working on yourself can be challenging when no one is rooting for you or when your hustle is misunderstood. So root for yourself and congratulate yourself on reaching your markers. You know how hard it is to be great, so embrace your resilience. Onlookers will be asking you how you did it once the hard work is done.

One of the greatest returns I know of from reaching any goal, month to month, is the accountability. You alone are responsible for your future. When you set out to accomplish a project and actually get it done, that's true power. Power is personal, and achievements come from keen focus and commitment. Keeping yourself in check and sticking to a long-term goal is always something to be proud of.

They say the most attractive thing about a woman is her confidence. I agree. The most confident people in a room are often the most comfortable too.

If you take note of the leaders, chairs, and

presidents of many top businesses, you might notice that they are commonly white and male. The opportunity for women to move up the pipeline of operations isn't always simple to obtain due to a lack of appointment and a lack of faith in our leadership.

The lack of visibility of women in this space causes a real problem, because its effects trickle down to the next generation. Not seeing a mature version of yourself in a field can be unstimulating and uninspiring. This can result in a lack of confidence or hesitancy in young girls to assert themselves in these environments.

If not for yourself, then for the sake of dismantling a biased, hierarchical system of gender oppression and exclusion, I urge you to maintain confidence on your journey to success, no matter what you pursue. So what if you're one of the few women who have trekked your path? What value does scrutiny and someone else's lack of confidence in you really hold? Your confidence and impact will speak for itself. Your presence alone may be all it takes for others to come through. Being first may be better than being last.

When you project confidence and positivity into the world, people will not take the same liberties with you as they will with someone who seems intimidated. Even more, when you are sure of yourself, there isn't much people can say to you that will take you out of your element.

With heightened confidence, words like *cannot* and *not allowed* are fictitious restrictions that apply only to the unmotivated or unconfident, not to you. Just because someone else cannot or has not doesn't mean you will not.

Develop a powerful sense of confidence, and know that the difficulty of many tasks is overstated. Once you realize that you can do anything you put your mind to, you will achieve your greatest dreams. There is always room to grow and improve, so forbid complacency in your life. Always think, want, and achieve more.

Another habit aligned with confidence is to resist declaring that you might not have the answer to a question, challenge, or task. You don't need to know the answer to everything in life; typically, you don't even need to know how to get the thing done. You just need to be unfazed, motivated, and confident enough to try, using the available resources. Next time you think you don't know or can't do something, I enjoin you to develop your ideas further. Use your resources and your mind to consider new possibilities for solutions. Assert your knowledge of general principles and apply them to fixed concepts. Even if you're wrong, you'll be content with your resilience and efforts.

To tone up your confidence, follow five

essential tips:

1. Be hyperaware of how social media affects you. Social media is a phenomenal tool when used properly. It can be a place to get inspired or inspire others, explore your creativity, support people, build a brand, and make friends. While there are great advantages and a lot of valuable content on social media, it can also stunt your productivity and induce self-doubt when used senselessly. Ask yourself these questions the next time you go for a scroll:

How does who I follow contribute to my life?

_____

Do the posts I see change my mood?

_____

Do they improve my mood?

_____

Am I comparing myself?

_____

Is this affecting my mental health?

_____

Excessive time on social media can be taxing. There's a lot to keep up with. Your confidence is heavily correlated with the opinions you hold of yourself. Your self-worth should not be based on social standards or comparisons with the images people post of only half of their lives. The good is glorified on these platforms and the reality is submerged. For this reason it's nice to admire aspects of people, but you must acknowledge that everyone has their own journey and starting place. This brings me to my second point.

2. Identify your strengths and capitalize on them. Sometimes we forget how great we are, especially when we're not actually trying to be great. Sometimes we just live. We don't always act out of hope for recognition or praise. When you're seeking confidence, knowing what sets you apart from the crowd will amplify your advantages and opportunities. Ask yourself:

What is something that people come to me for?

_____

What's one area in my life that I have a good handle on?

_____

How have I developed my _____ (*a strength that you inhibit*), and how has that improved who I am, all around?

_____

What sets me apart from the rest?

_____

3. Fake it till you make it. Training or tricking yourself into being confident is a great way to boost your self-confidence. When you're uncertain, do you find yourself looping the last word of your sentence to make your point into a question? Say what you mean, and mean what you say. They always say, *Dress for the role you want.* If you want to be more confident, speak affirmatively, stand tall, make eye contact, loosen your jaw, and walk with purpose. You'll find that if you sound confident, people often will believe you are, and you'll soon start thinking so too. Consider the following:

What tendencies do I have when I feel unconfident? *(Minimized opinions or comments, stuttering, increased heart rate?)*

How can I prevent this or control these habits?

What triggers me to feel unconfident?

_____

How can I counter my response and overcome this?

_____

4. Eliminate negative self-talk. Get out of your own way. Sometimes the biggest force acting against you is yourself. If you can see it in your mind, you can become it or build it. You have so much to offer and you are special because you are you. That is your power. You had that thought, you have the drive, and you have the confidence. Hush any contrary thoughts. Consider these questions:

Does my negative self-talk reflect what I assume others think of me?

_____

Do I feel a certain way because **once**, in the past, things didn't work out as I planned?

_____

Why am I dismissing my strengths and potential, despite the fact that I am amazing?

---

5. Never forget that you are the boss. It's normal not to be aware of your own superiority when you're faced with an interview, a conversation, a business transaction, or just about any other interpersonal exchange. But what we often overlook is that the other person in these interactions requires and depends on our comments and responses. That means you're in charge. You meet all the credentials for the job—that's why you applied. You've done your research—that's why you're ready to commit. You've combed through your thoughts and that's why you're ready to respond.

The conversations you engage in are owned 50% by you and rely 100% on your responses. Use your words wisely, grace others with your confidence, show them why you are essential, and let them hear why your words matter. Do you ever wonder about the following?

What is the vision I have of my present self?

_____

In what ways am I in control of my life?

_____

How can I reframe my life so that I'm in charge of me?

_____

Assert yourself and keep yourself at the forefront of your life. We have an instinctive inclination to seek meaningful connections with others; we like what we like and who we like. The people we love most understand our weirdness, comfort us in our sadness, and reinforce the beauty of our uniqueness. We care for others as we would like others to care for us.

Company and companionship are blessings. A good family and cherished friends are not as common as you might think. As with anything else in life, we must work to nurture and develop promising and healthy relationships if we want a lasting bond.

It's crucial never to take a backseat in these interconnections. To inherit a beautiful, full, successful life, you must value yourself highly enough to know that you cannot benefit others if you haven't learned to benefit yourself. Never compromise on who you are becoming.

As beautiful as the first flower of spring is, I hope you don't pick it. Let it bloom. The best is yet to come. Nurture it and tend to its needs, and let it show you what it's meant to do.

You are growing and glowing more with every passing day. You are a work in progress, a budding flower, a butterfly ready to break out of its cocoon. Surge upward again and allow yourself a second chance, another opportunity to live fully on your terms. Become your own woman.

Prioritize yourself, because you deserve it. Devoting yourself to working on you above all else will not only be personally fulfilling, others will reap the benefit of knowing the best you that can exist. Putting yourself first allows you to create a more pure, pleasurable, and structured experience of life.

Whatever you truly want out of life, I encourage you to go get it. Set your goals and intentionally attain them. It's the passion and pure desire within us that makes our daily work worthwhile.

On the eternal quest to discovering who you are, it is essential to establish why you want to succeed in what you want to succeed. Determine your what and your why. Your what will become your goals, and your why will become your purpose. Together, these will strengthen your commitment to your life.

Understanding the reasons behind your motives for success will give you a sense of fulfillment and a better understanding of yourself. This understanding will connect you to your purpose. Your purpose will be what ensures your real happiness.

Knowing the why behind your intentions will also connect you to your goals on an emotional level. Your purpose in pursuing your goals can bring you joy and pride and it can release anger or resentment. This emotional connection creates an additional responsibility for you that will enhance your dedication.

Your resurgence as a new you begins with realizing who you were always inclined to be. As long as you are doing what you want to be doing, and not what you're expected to do, you are en route to being your own woman, an individual, a boss.

The hardest part of the journey is often the beginning, but you don't have to wait until the end for the best part. The rising action, struggle, triumphs, and successes of your life are what will be your most cherished, vivid, and proud memories.

Your success story is in the works right now.

Maybe you haven't acknowledged everything you've overcome or how far you've traveled. Or maybe you feel that you haven't gotten very far at all. But either way, you're not starting at square one. You are revising, improving, and dominating your own life in pursuit of personal success. Your journey, whether you're starting school or finishing it, joining a business or establishing one, losing twenty pounds or helping others help themselves, will not be a straight line, nor will it be simple. But I promise that committing to yourself and living to ensure your own happiness will be the best investment of your life. The most valuable things you can learn are about yourself, your capabilities, and your purpose.

I learned about myself the hard way. In my sophomore year of college, I had a full blackout moment. It's not what you're thinking—there were no tequila or jello shots. There was no party at all, in fact. In the moment I'm describing, all the lights, of my inner self just powered off. There was darkness, stillness, and then silence. But once my inner light came back on, everything started to click.

At this time, I was exhausted from forcing friendships that I didn't feel were warmly harmonious. I was uninterested in routinely putting myself in rooms where I felt out of place, not only socially but in my own body. Most importantly, I felt an emptiness in operating with an uncertain vision of who I was, which resulted in losing myself trying to fit into molds that were not carved for me. I was filled to capacity with self-doubt.

Soren Kierkegaard once wrote, *Life can only be understood backwards, but it must be lived forwards*. I know now that the reason I felt so astray in my own body was that I'd made a poor outline of who I was and I was resistant to uncovering who I was destined to be. I lacked goals, I felt guilty for putting myself first, and my confidence was absent and inexplicably mislaid.

In my frustration with feeling so foreign in my own body, I had to consider this: When you lose your keys, you actively go searching for them so that you can leave where you are and get to where you need to be. The same applies to your life. How can you expect to find yourself without actively searching?

I had to condition myself to abandon the mindset that I must please others and gain their acceptance. The mind is powerful at filling in assumptions in the space between your thoughts and the thoughts of others. Just like the brain has a hard time distinguishing between what you see with your eyes and what you see in your mind, sometimes it's not what people say that messes with our understanding, but what we think they mean.

Allowing the judgments and assumptions of

others to impede your thoughts and actions is counterproductive and senseless. There is no benefit in striving for approval or winning someone's acceptance of you. Live unapologetically and for those who approve; that's good for them. For the rest, there will always be naysayers and people who project their frustrations with their own insufficiencies onto you. There will also be people who plainly just will not root for you. Some individuals are not capable of being happy for you. So live for yourself. You can only be concerned with your own thoughts and the motivations behind your own actions and behaviors.

We all need moments in our lives when we take a step back, maybe even have a "blackout" moment, and re-center ourselves. We all go through periods when we're confused about how to take the next step. Some of us are even confused about how we reached the present moment, both in positive and negative ways: *Things might have been so much better before*, or *things would be so great if only. . . .* These torpid periods are actually a beautiful marker of your success. They ignite self-reflection and become the embarkation points for new beginnings.

Countering your lack of confidence, lack of goals, or lack of commitment to putting yourself first is the key to success. Are you going to understand your life from inside a cage, viewing your goals as out of reach and intractable? Or will you acknowledge that all you ever needed has always been within reach? It's always been inside of you. It's in your confidence. It's in your goals. It's in putting yourself first.

You are one decision away from an incredible life. It's up to you to define who you are and who you will become. You might as well make her amazing.

REDEFINE YOUR AMAZING

What does being in control of your life mean to you?

_____

_____

_____

To achieve your goals, where do you need to
minimize your distractions?

_____

_____

_____

In conquering your personal victories, is there
anything you feel challenged by?

_____

_____

_____

How will you overcome this and arise bigger than
your concerns and fears?

_____

_____

_____

Become Your <u>Own</u> *Woman*

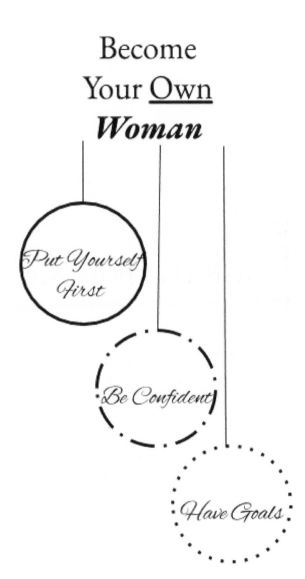

Put Yourself First

Be Confident

Have Goals

3 | NICE TO MEET ME

Here's what happened when I found myself unemployed with a stray dog following me around Cuba. To set the scene, I was one thousand, three hundred, and seventeen miles south of my home in New Jersey, in the middle of June. I was also on the twenty-sixth day of what would turn out to be a ninety-day period without a job. This meant no work, no pay, and it seemed to me, no meaning. The reasons for my circumstances are less interesting than the virtue of the story: what happened during my time in Havana was an alteration of my mind. I found comfort in an overprotective domestic hound, lightness in living unconventionally, and acceptance in the flow of life's changes.

I've come to understand that the only constant in life is change. Time changes every second, every minute another baby is born, every day the moon shifts in its rotation, and every year, when you reflect on yourself, you'll find that you're more different than the same. But I'm not sure if this is the same kind of change. Your change is a result of moving closer to who you are destined to become.

Your value is far greater than your position at your job. You are more than an employee, or even a partner, more than your degree or even your title, and more than somebody's daughter or even someone's mother. Your value is greater than your salary, your shortcomings, or your relationships. The only constant in all of the roles you play in life is you, the raw version of you. Unloading who you are is no simple task, because you are, have been, and will always be different figures in your own life.

Sometimes it takes an out-of-body experience or a gander in the mirror to recognize that you will be ok. I was in Cuba after finishing college and didn't have a job. I thought the worst of myself, my capabilities, my goals, and my circumstances. I spent hours applying for jobs, and when I took a break I used it to wallow in frustration. What would have been more fruitful was using my break to just breathe, pray, and relieve myself of the pressures I'd placed on my mind.

Among all of life's changes, the one that is most reliably consistent is that your worst days will come to an end, your best days are not so far away, and all will eventually subside. The best place to be during times of opposition is in the present. There is no sense in being bothered by what has happened in the past; you can't change it. Why trouble yourself with anxiety about the future? You can't perfectly predict it. For now, just be present.

We all follow independent paths through life. Very few people are truly similar, because who we are depends largely on who we've been, what we've done, and how we've changed. The smallest decisions we make can be the biggest deterrents or accelerants in our lives.

Life, especially the decisions we make within it, is not something we should deem regretful, not the positive choices we make nor the negative outcomes that we encounter. The series of decisions, actions, and stories that makes up life are far too great to want to rescind. Your biggest mistakes and failures will morph into some of your greatest moments.

Coming into the world, we're crying, screaming even, while others are rejoicing in the beginning of our lives. When we become sick with a cough, stuffy nose, or chills we're bothered, frustrated, and weak—yet ironically, our immune system deserves praise for its increased strength in overcoming a cold. We scrape our knees and suffer in anger after falling off our bikes. But not long afterward, we get back on with heightened confidence and determination. Life is full of messages that reveal to us who we are, who we can become, and the beauty in our struggles. Yet we're quick to be frustrated at our situations without realizing that beyond them lie amazing triumphs. We can be so preoccupied with self-doubt while our potential is perfectly evident to others. We are gifted with so many royalties and perks that we overlook the fact that we have the keys to success and we just need to use them.

Some of our most prized moments develop out of unfavorable situations. These are the events that make our talents, brilliance, and innovation evident. Dissatisfaction is one of the strongest forces for enthusing us to grow and find greater meaning in our lives. You can stay angry at your situation, or you can change it.

Overcoming a mental difficulty, whether it's anxiety, depression, or some other internal force, is a very tough fight. These trials are not uncommon, nor are they to be disregarded as insignificant. Mental struggles, though tough, can be conquered with the right help from external forces but most importantly, from within yourself. Change doesn't happen unless you do.

Don't pass your mental health off as a second-class concern. Acknowledge when you need to take a step back to re-center yourself. Seek help and take things slowly.

If you're in pain, what brought you comfort today? List something small or large.

_____

How will tomorrow be better?

_____

Allow yourself to regain control of your life and put yourself and your needs first.

Sometimes the things that trigger our poor mental health and make us feel insufficient are things that work themselves out. Just breathe. Try to focus on what's most important *right now*. Let the past stay in the past, and let's live in the present as we approach the future.

We all want to be happy, and happiness is attainable through alignment with our purpose. Beneath all the things that make us different from one another and from who we used to be is a single uniting force that guides us back to why we do what we do: We all have the innate desire to expose our life's purpose and seek out answers in our individual searches for meaning. Have you ever wondered if there was deeper meaning behind the messages and actions of your life? I find these moments to be subtle glimpses into our purpose. When you feel something resonate within you and you have butterflies in your stomach, lean in. Follow the message. It's a stepping stone towards your purpose.

◆◆◆

Taking care of yourself—and knowing when it's necessary to do so—is a part of personal competence. Try to take at least one hour a day to maintain your sanity, unplug from the noise, rejuvenate your soul, and cater to your personal needs. You may be busy but think of it as just sixty minutes, thirty-six hundred seconds, or as less than 5% of your day. You deserve that much.

Take the time to develop, reconstruct, and sustain a healthy mind. Your days will be brighter and lighter once you've tuned into yourself. Your mind, body, and soul are calling you. You need to respond and nurture your temple and make sure you are balanced.

Be receptive to your thoughts, feelings, words, and actions. Be willing to accept signs from within yourself that may not be obvious. When a situation doesn't feel right, the energy will be off and you will feel uninterested, annoyed, or maybe confused. Your inner knowing signals when something is not right. Conceptualize the issue. If a situation isn't elevating you, teaching you, or bringing you positivity, it may not be for you.

Another way of observing your own mind is by understanding your emotions. Take the time to figure out where your emotions come from and why they exist. Knowing what makes you happy and why it makes you happy will put your true values in the proper perspective. Realizing what makes you stressed and why you find it stressful will also make your lack of interest in various things clear. Your tolerance will also be revealed.

Intense emotions have the potential to shape your actions. It is best to make decisions rationally and clear of emotional bias. For this reason, taking quiet moments to be still and figure yourself out will let you find guidance, insight, and clarity that might save you from poor choices or regretful words.

Even when you find yourself surrounded by others, take time for yourself. Prioritize and love yourself enough to set boundaries. I purposefully emphasize how vital it is to put yourself first, not selfishly but selflessly. Let this serve as your reminder that you weren't brought into this world to be placed second, especially not in your own life.

In being cognizant of your mind's tendencies, you will be more aware of the dark, negative places your mind may lurk. When you repeatedly think that you aren't good enough, you'll make yourself miss out on the best opportunities. You are in control of your thoughts and your destiny. Catch yourself when you notice that you're pulling back from the positive.

You are the initiator of your success. Acknowledging your bad habits is essential for optimal growth. Once you are aware of these patterns, you will become more powerful than them and can decide how to eliminate them.

When you aren't conscious of your negative self-talk and thinking, you may be oblivious as to why you miss opportunities and fail to achieve your goals. Don't be the reason you are held back from happiness and success.

Remember not to allow society to hold you back either. In my opinion, mental traps like the reminder that women need to work three times as hard as men, are just attempts to block our successes. Nudges like that are just exasperating. Women, people of color, minorities, and other historically oppressed groups are often expected to enlighten the world and our oppressors about their assertion of power and how it brings harm to the rest of society.

If we were to remind ourselves daily that we have to work three times as hard and also explain how the odds are stacked against us to the people that are stacking those odds, I don't know how many of us would even want to get up. I advise you not to concentrate so adamantly on hardships but to move toward opportunity and potential. Work to bring your dreams and aspirations to life on your own terms, regardless of who is rooting for you or against you.

Women are born to stand out, not fit in, anyway. But this will only happen when we accept ourselves as the perfect outliers. Be the one who works harder, not because she has to but because she knows that only her personal best is good enough and that there is no basis for holding back talent and strength.

If you are complacent in the knowledge that elements are systematically against you and make no movement toward change, when will the cycle culminate? How will your circumstances ever change?

Problems do not get resolved on their own. That requires purposeful action. Solutions are what fix problems. Shape the future and rid your daughters and further descendants of the excuses, burdens, and circumstances that have halted women today and in the days that preceded us.

Create the opportunities you desire. Don't wait for them to be handed out; take responsibility for your fate. Your purpose is unlike anyone else's. For that reason, there is no competition. Competition insists that there must be a winner, but we can all win when we focus on what we personally desire. You don't need to take from others to get ahead, and you do need to realize what's yours is only for you.

Your aspirations aren't one-size-fits-all.

Receiving the best opportunities and fulfilling your life begins with how you understand yourself and the world in your mind. In seeking a deeper understanding of your mind, ask yourself:

Do I understand my emotions?

_____

Do I speak positively to myself?

_____

Do I allow past frustrations to affect my thoughts and feelings even after I'm physically removed from the situation?

_____

How can I actively refuse this response and instead maintain peace in these situations?

_____

The complement to obtaining a healthy mind is catering to your body's needs. This goes beyond exercise, though a nice workout is always a good start. It's very difficult to be consumed by external worries while running on a steep incline at a whirlwind pace.

Physical activity is an amazing escape and way to reset your energy. A moderate walk outdoors or a light swim is a good way to re-center yourself while appreciating your surroundings, your abilities, and your peace.

Exercise is relaxing to the mind because it often requires you to be in the present. Only focusing on the now relieves stress both from the mind and the body.

Yoga, massages, and meditation all allow your mind to calm down and catch up with itself. When you get out of shape, you make time for the gym. When you smell ripe at the end of the day, you shower. Likewise, when your mind is working overtime, you take care of your brain and mental energy. The result of your detox is a clear mind that is ready to make optimal decisions and think rationally.

Though you will feel revitalized through physical activity, your body may also feel reinvigorated from a good night's sleep. A fully shut-down period of relaxation is essential to sustaining a pristine, healthy, and functional you.

Getting enough sleep is simple, yet it is often

overlooked. Resting gives your body and your mind a much-needed break. It's good to give yourself ample time for rejuvenation before taking on each new day. When your car's gas tank is approaching empty, you fill it up. Hold yourself to the same standard: revitalize yourself. You'll make better decisions from a clear mind and a serene body after you take a hiatus.

Letting your body recharge will reward you with a steadier flow of productivity. The best choices don't depend just on knowledge but on knowing yourself and understanding your emotions. This is best done with routine self-care checks from making time for what you deeply enjoy to taking a moment to rest in silence.

Listening to your body by way of deep breathing can also help you achieve peace of mind. Focusing on deep inhales and exhales allows you to reconsider your quick reactions and respond with a level head. It's like clicking a reset button.

To arrive at the best method for nurturing your body, ask yourself:

How many hours of sleep did I get last night? Is this ideal? If not, how many hours will I strive for?

What outlets or activities do I enjoy that allow me to get out of my own head?

_____

What are my favorite ways to decompress at the end of the day?

_____

How do I practice self-care?

_____

Getting in tune with your soul requires you to be heavily intuitive and active in listening to your inner being. Tapping into your soul will allow clarity to flow in and the unnecessary to wash away. Some of our knowledge and thoughts are instinctual. Listen to yourself and take control of your own life, body, and mind.

The soul is the part of us that craves to know the meaning of our lives. We can get in tune with our souls through self-reflection, prayer, meditation, and connection to certain songs and various forms of art.

Choose to be inactive sometimes. When you're resting and get past the urge to use your phone, pause for a few minutes. Relax and clear your mind. See where it goes, but understand it through an observational lens. What values and virtues do you hold dearly and carry daily? How do they affect the way you interpret your life? Self-reflection and understanding are at the foundation of inner peace and acknowledging who you truly are.

Your soul, mind, and body are intertwined. When you work toward personal success and fulfillment, you can't work on mastering your body alone and neglect your mind. You cannot feel the utmost connectivity to your soul yet have no concern with the health of your body.

We are our bodies, our minds, and our souls. We are the presentation of our wellness, thoughts, and virtues. Don't neglect to tone the aspects of your being that need work or attention. Our wholeness arrives when these three components are fulfilled as well. In search of a more solid understanding of your soul, ask yourself:

What practices can I perform to get in tune with my soul?

_____

What values do I hold dearly?

_____

When was the last time I reflected on my life
and who I am?

_____

How can I actively make time for this?

_____

Getting to know yourself by comprehending your
mind, body, and soul will grant you advantages
beyond the personal. When you realize who you are,
it will be clear to others also. When someone is unfit
to love you the way you love yourself, you'll have
the strength and sense to move forward on your life's
quest.

Self-love and understanding motivate you to
make healthy choices. When you hold yourself in
high esteem, you're more likely to choose things that
nurture and serve you well—healthy eating, exercise,
or simply preserving good relationships.

Self-love is the best love, the most important
love, and the only love you need. Need, not want:
how can you expect anyone to love you if you can't
love yourself? You don't need another half to make
you whole. Be whole within yourself.

Self-love will encourage you to refuse
insecurities. One of the greatest treasures I gained

from getting to know myself fully and personally was disallowing insecurities to define me as they once had.

I used to instinctively wonder what people thought of me as I approached them. My amplified social awareness and yearning to figure out how others perceived me grew out of predetermined generalizations or stereotypes. I would first analyze how I imagined others saw me: Simple. A black girl. Whether for good or for ill, my social identity would serve as my introduction before I could even utter my name.

Growing up as a young, black girl in the suburbs, my mind operated in two modes. One mode allowed me to be free, let my curly hair out, get more glow from a day at the beach, and be as loud as I wanted.

The other mode operated in accordance with my conscience. My conscience would ring out a constant reminder that no one else's hair was like mine, so I should straighten it. It constantly nudged me to remember that when all my classmates returned from the beach, they'd be closer to my color, so if I didn't want to stand out even more than I already did, I should stay inside. It gave me a constant poke to note that if I made too much noise, the other kids would claim that black girls are always so loud, so I should stay quiet.

This is how social preconceptions contributed to who I was: a quiet, light-skinned, black girl with chemically-straightened-hair.

Who we are is widely understood through who the world believes us to be. Society may see you one way, but you are or can be another. Know that you can be more. Embrace your attributes, and let society waste its breath on its false depiction of you.

I am proud and blessed not just to be a woman but to be a black woman. I think these particular aspects of my intersectionality are what make me better. I get to look like a brown glazed donut in the summer and enjoy sorrel at Christmastime in the winter. My hair can go from a curly wash-and-go to flat-iron straight, to box braids arranged with kanekalon hair, and everything in between. I choose to embrace my black womanhood.

Love yourself and know yourself for who you understand yourself to be. Allow your mind, body, and soul to direct and illustrate who you are through an analysis of how you feel. You are a premium distinction. All you ever needed to succeed in life has been in your mind, heart, and soul since the beginning. Embrace and understand yourself fully and you will find a more fulfilling life.

TAKE YOURSELF PERSONALLY

How do you define peace?

_____
_____
_____

Do you typically attend to or ignore the messages
your body relays to your mind?

_____
_____
_____

When do you feel you are at the greatest peace
within yourself?

_____
_____
_____

What benefits and power come with getting in touch
with your inner self?

_____
_____
_____

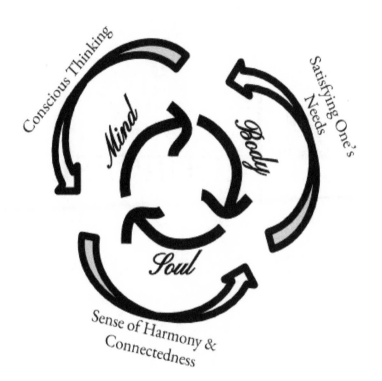

4 | EQUIPOISE

Burgers and fries, pens and paper, washers and dryers. These pairs just make sense. Hot, crispy, salted fries served with a fat, juicy burger makes a dinner whole. A clean sheet of paper torn from a notebook gives a bold ballpoint pen purpose. The hot, sturdy dryer waits to perform after the washer to complete a hefty laundry cycle. These basic, agreeable combinations make for a great meal, trustworthy notes, and clean clothes. They go hand-in-hand because each item gives the other purpose; they make each other whole.

Another basic yet essential combination is between your most powerful, fierce self and the virtuous pursuit of personal fulfillment. When you shift the focus of your life to ensuring that you will evolve into the greatest you can be, you will find an unshakable confidence in yourself. You will know yourself well and be more mindful of where you exert your energy and who is worthy of receiving it.

Once you make yourself a priority, you will find a powerful ability to balance your destiny with your external relationships. You will find this in three ways:

1. By having the capacity to make the best decisions for yourself.
2. By focusing more on what you have and less on what you lack.
3. By being less consumed by the future and more focused on the present.

Balancing your personal fate with your external relationships is essential to your growth on your journey to fulfillment. You need to observe a healthy balance between loving and putting yourself first and loving and prioritizing others. This balance will allow only the most exemplary people to join you on your journey.

We all need support and love from others to experience the fullness of life. There are some lessons and joys that can only be found in our relationships with others. Who you spend your time with, who you prioritize, and who you develop feelings for play a substantial role in who you become. These people will inhibit or encourage your progress and motivate or minimize your accomplishments. The energy and influences you allow around you will affect you considerably, so choose wisely.

The people in your circle should be uplifting,

warm, and positive. Your relationships should be equally harmonious. If those around you aren't adding to your life, they're taking up space or sapping your energy. You want to be filled up with knowledge, love, laughter, and life, not drained of them. Make sure the people you invite on your journey can help you illuminate the world along the way.

This is why it is so important to understand yourself first and build this healthy balance. It would be counterproductive to put so much effort into building the best, most confident you only to be held back by others who are unwilling to do the same for themselves. Surround yourself with forward-thinking, growth-minded people. Don't entertain stagnancy in your life, not within yourself and not within others.

Unproductivity can be contagious when you're around it. Motivating yourself around the unmotivated is challenging, because there will always be more reasons to do nothing than to do something. You wouldn't want that for yourself, and if you don't want it for the people in your flock, encourage them to seek more. Be the leader, be the light.

The search for fulfillment is a never-ending, yet treasurable journey. It's a voyage of upward movements, bountiful challenges, and endless accomplishments. That's why it's necessary to enjoy the journey. Long for the voyage, because once you arrive at your destination, another journey will be waiting. You can always be greater, but make sure you pause and reflect on your successes with rapture.

Similarly, you won't find personal success living a life in which your sole purpose is to help someone else's dream come true. Practice compassion and hard work. Help others, but be sure to help yourself too. In your evolution, if it cannot be your main focus just yet, it is paramount to have a side hustle or hobby. That's where you'll find and build on your purpose.

If it's not for monetary ends, use your hobby as a creative outlet. Develop something you're great at, and add your personal touch. Get better every day, and take note of the principles that lead to your happiness and prosperity.

If your side hustle does bring you compensation, you should still see it as a creative outlet. Doing something you love, something you're amazing at, and something that helps others all in one will bring you great fulfillment. Once you can monetize your side project, make it your main hustle. Don't limit yourself to fulfilling someone else's dream—you're capable of so much more.

◆◆◆

The glory of owning your confidence, putting yourself first, and striving for your goals will make you a woman who doesn't have time for any nonsense. Your capacity to choose the best relationships will be so pristine that you may shock yourself. Holding yourself to a higher standard will make it simpler and clearer to weed out the people who aren't worth your time. You won't tolerate nonsensical people who are not committed, consistent, uplifting, or at the bare minimum, motivated.

There's no shame in rejecting what isn't for you. If you know that someone isn't serious or devoted to building with you when you're seeking commitment, don't waste your time. Your time is valuable, and your energy is too. Don't waste it on those who are undeserving.

Likewise, you should never have to minimize yourself for the sake of others. If you're heavily invested in building a beautiful future for yourself, you'll be busy and motivated. Being with someone who can't grasp the magnitude of such a goal and lifestyle can stunt your productivity. Find someone who gets you, understands your drive, and has big goals for herself or himself. Hold yourself to a higher standard. Insist that people who aren't on your level find their way up there, because you're not willing to minimize your magnitude.

Respect for yourself and integrity will make you an unstoppable force. A partner should not lead to you stopping or changing your motivations, methods, or goals. Great integrity requires that you stick to what you set out to do. Love, respect, and discipline yourself enough to continue your journey at all costs.

When you make better choices, you'll soon realize that you've created a VIP section within your own life. This won't come from arrogance or disdain, but simply because you will be much more particular about who can gain access to you.

How you feel is a reflection of how you think. How you think is a reflection of how you feel. Consume positivity in all areas of your life and that will be reflected in your everyday emotions, thoughts, and actions.

Your arrival at a healthy, balanced relationship is rooted in self-love. You must love yourself wholeheartedly before you can expect to properly give others love or receive it from them. Self-love stems from knowing your own worth, which surfaces once you prioritize yourself. The way you love yourself will teach others how to love you.

The decisions you make in pursuit of a balanced relationship often arise from gut feelings. When you possess considerable intelligence and a strong emotional intelligence, you are better able to perceive and encode information without trying. This subliminal perception can be thought of as your gut feeling. Emotional intelligence is the ability to notice and understand emotions in yourself and in others, and to use this understanding to manage your behavior and relationships. There's immense power in acknowledging and understanding how your moods affect your thoughts and decisions. There are also bountiful advantages in doing the same for others.

Your subliminal perceptions and judgements shouldn't be brushed aside. They offer a good opportunity to trace the sources of your feelings and thoughts. When your gut tells you that something is off, figure out why you feel that way. Trust your intuition, but also rummage through the assumption. Recollect the path you took to arrive at this conclusion, and consider communicating it to the individual at the root of your divide.

All relationships require work from both parties, even the ones that seem like they don't. We must actively improve ourselves and realize that we need to get better because we all have faults. Though it's imprudent to ignore red flags, you also have to remember that you can't judge people for their choices when you don't know what options they had to choose from, what circumstances they were in, or what outdated version of themselves they were. We aren't all dealt the same hands in life, so remember that no one grew up with exactly the same experiences as you. Limit your judgements, consider your intuition, but also empathize.

Empathy is a special skill that lets us glimpse our knowledge through the resistance of our own egos when we're trying to discern another person's world. Use your emotional intellect to identify who the person is and how they became the person they are.

You'll never find someone who is perfect, and you'll never be perfect either. We're all flawed to some degree, and that's fine. It is not "settling" to accept someone who is largely but not entirely what you desire. The most powerful trait in a partner is their potential and drive. Given what they lack, do they have the drive to accomplish more? For all they have, do they have the drive for more? Ask yourself:

What standards do I hold for my partner?

_____

What standards do I hold for myself?

_____

How often do I listen to my gut?

_____

Do I consider both my logical thinking and my intuition when making a decision?

_____

Hold the people in your life to the same standard you hold yourself or to a higher one. If you choose to hold them to a higher standard, let that be your reminder to never stop growing. Understand that you're worthy of loving and being loved. Know that you can't always expect, but you can always share. Align yourself with people who fill you with a love as great as the love with which you fill yourself. When you find someone you can join your life to, live in the moment. Enjoy the micro-moments, savor the mega-milestones, and take note of the thoughts that surface in affectionate words and the actions that follow them.

As annoying as it can be to hear *Enjoy being single*, do enjoy it and optimize this framework of your life. Groom yourself to find the blessings in your life every day. When you are confident and happy in your life, you will feel yourself coming full circle to who you were always destined to be. Your life will make sense.

Don't overlook solitude. In your free time, observe the beauty in seclusion and peace. For some reason, people believe that they need company at all times. That's not conducive to growth or self-reflection. The value of clarity and peace is greatly overlooked.

Some people assume that singlehood is synonymous with loneliness, sorrow, and boredom. Flip the script and disregard this view. Don't let others decide how you should feel and think. Think as an individual. Stay true to you.

A relationship will not define your life. Live your life fully, vibrantly, and energetically. You don't need a partner to be complete. You don't need a partner because all your friends have partners. Thinking you do is the recipe for a rushed, half-baked decision that may leave you in an awful situation.

Do not settle. Remind yourself of why you want what you want. Do you want someone just for the satisfaction of being in a relationship, or do you want a meaningful connection? Seek to please yourself. Be patient until you come across someone whose values and standards align with yours. Let life unfold naturally. Don't allow the false emergencies you create in your mind to rush the perfect timing of your life.

Find strength in self-sufficiency. When you reflect on your thoughts and actions, you'll find a genuine understanding of yourself. It will be clear which behaviors are natural to you and which are conditioned responses to the company of others. You'll begin to create pure, genuine thoughts while improving on your independence.

Enhance your creativity. Operate on your own time, develop your thoughts fully, and practice doing exactly what you want to do, when you want to do it.

Intentionally spend more time with yourself to understand yourself better. Turn your thoughts into ideas and your ideas into projects. Arrange your time to work on something you've been incessantly putting off. Write in your journal or write a book. Establish a side hustle or a business. Find a new hobby, spend more time with your friends, plan a trip, or date casually. Think about your strengths, and optimize them. Reflect on your faults, and flip them into fixes. Simply be productive and make good use of the time you have. This will lead to some of your greatest accomplishments.

Be active and alert in your search for a partner, if that's what you seek, but don't be consumed by it. Things will work out in your benefit as long as you strive adamantly to see the best in all facets of life.

Realize the power of your mind and your thoughts. What you think evolves into how you feel, how you feel is often understood through how you act, and this becomes responsible for what you receive. You can't dwell on what you don't have and expect that to grant you what you desire.

The best you can do is live for today and make who you are even greater, primarily for yourself and secondarily for whoever will be in your life today and in the future. Worrying about not being with someone will only taint your mind by making you think you're incomplete. You are not. By remaining calm and true to who you are, you'll develop a trust that everything will be alright, which it will. Be patient, and shift your focus and energy to now.

When we take a few steps back and look at the grand concept of our dearest desires, we are called to recognize that forcing them will only make them break. We ruin opportunities when we refuse to handle them delicately. When you allow the events and relationships in your life to occur naturally, you become more serene, you let yourself think reasonably, and you focus on the more important things.

Embrace all forms of your life. Life is about

perspective. Catch yourself from falling into the trap of *I'll be happy when. . . .* Acknowledge your habits of postponing happiness until your next accomplishment. If you always put off your happiness until next time, when do you expect to enjoy what's right in front of you? You have to be happy in the present and enjoy the motions of your life. Ask yourself:

What are three things that have made me happy this month?

What are three things that have made me happy this week?

What are three things that have made me happy today?

Elect yourself to be the designator of your joy. When you are constantly searching for love, happiness, or acceptance, you fail to acknowledge everything that you have. You have more to be happy about and proud of than you give yourself credit for.

Owning your happiness will transform you into a better friend and partner. Positivity and happiness are magnetic. Ask yourself:

What am I most grateful for?

_____

What is my favorite part of spending time with myself?

_____

Do I embrace periods of solitude?

_____

Do I embrace my life regardless of my relationship status?

_____

Find peace within yourself and confidence in the unveiling of your life. There are few things outside ourselves that we can control entirely. When you're dealing with someone else, you have to realize that you do not have full control. You can plan and plan, but things will always be interpreted uniquely by each person, and life's unpredictability will run its course. Plans don't always unfold as you intend them to, but that's the beauty of life. It's also the beauty of partnership.

The value of partnership is in having someone to build with, bounce ideas off, or get a second opinion from. That's why it's important to only accept someone of considerable worth. You should crave someone who offers a beautiful perspective, an original opinion, and undying support.

When you have a like-minded, forward-thinking partner, you can build each other up on your journey toward your respective goals. Whether you share a goal or your goals are completely opposite of one another, it's beautiful to have a partner who understands your path or the dedication it takes to conquer something meaningful. Even better, you may have someone you can learn from and lean on. That person should help you tone up your weaknesses and crystalize your strengths.

In a harmonious relationship, it's important to resonate with your personal expressions of love. How do you show love? It's awesome to be loved and to feel warmth from a partner. But we shouldn't expect more than we are willing to give. Make sure you do your part. You only have control over yourself, so live up to your responsibility by making sure you know how to love properly. It is a unique and powerful thing to be able to embrace individuality in togetherness. Living as two separate individuals who are united in common feelings toward one another is not as commonplace as you'd think.

Stay true to your path and embrace who you are fully. Your individuality is what makes your partnerships unique and sustainable. We become even greater when we work together. But you first have to do your part and adhere to the fullest life you can by seeking to fill yourself with greatness and understanding. Ask yourself:

How do I balance individuality in togetherness?

_____

What benefits come with partnership?

_____

What are my favorite ways to express love?

_____

How do I slow myself down and return to the present?

Placing yourself at the forefront of your life makes it easier to balance relationships with who you are becoming. Recognizing your own importance will be the biggest, boldest decision of your life. The choices you make from a place of confidence and happiness will reward you with people worthy of your energy and love. Knowing yourself will also allow you to appreciate what you already have while you await your pending blessings. Being balanced within will grant you equilibrium in the present and put you at peace with what is to come.

Devoting time to yourself and your success will reward you endlessly. It will open up a flow of personally manifested residual blessings in the form of wiser behavior, an improved mindset, and a dominating, boss-like aura. Love yourself enough to never compromise who you are. Keep adding to your greatness and getting closer to your purpose.

SEEK INDIVIDUALITY IN TOGETHERNESS

What does it mean to you to hold yourself to a higher standard?

_____

_____

What do you do in your free time?

_____

_____

How do you prioritize yourself when in a relationship?

_____

_____

List three things about yourself that you can control right now, in the present.

_____

_____

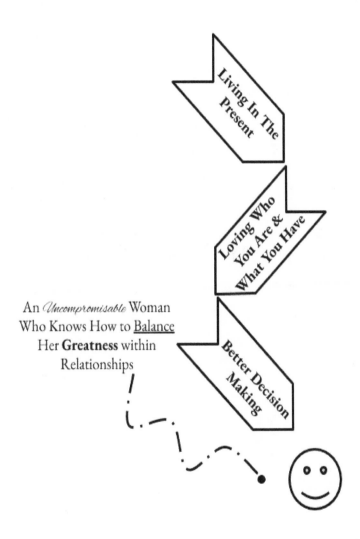

Living In The Present

Loving Who You Are & What You Have

Better Decision Making

An *Uncompromisable* Woman Who Knows How to <u>Balance</u> Her **Greatness** within Relationships

5 | SHE WHO WAS ME

I once woke up in a Walgreens, and it honestly wasn't the worst sleep of my life. Maybe the discomfort was worse than I remember, but that's beside the point.

I'd flown to Miami for spring break with about seven friends and we'd overlooked the fact that arriving at 10 PM the night before our hotel check-in would leave us stranded: apparently when they set our 3 PM check-in for the next day, they meant it. In any matter, after locating a late-night restaurant, taking shifts napping in the pharmacy area at the back of Walgreens, and finding other odd activities to pass the time, we did make it to our hotel. And somehow by the end of the trip, my memory recorded it as the best spring break of all time.

The first seventeen hours were rugged, though, to say the least (did I mention that I took a half-shower in the sink of the hotel lobby when we arrived early?). But I didn't allow this now-miniscule moment to impede the greatness and excitement that were there to be had. *Life is all about perspective.*

Finding happiness in the ordinary moments of life is essential when you're seeking a full and balanced life. Happiness is a choice. Life is unpredictable, and we are all imperfect. We must seek contentment with this truth and find the light in what is beyond our control. That's the best way to keep your peace.

Perfection is unlikely and oftentimes unnatural, and seeking it will not grant you peace. Live in a reasonable but challenging way. Doing your best will be your ultimate achievement.

Your personal best is what is good enough. Focusing too heavily on your missteps will distract you from your main goal. Though keeping yourself accountable is important, you must also acknowledge your progress and applaud yourself when you are nearing your goals, rather than dwelling on what you could have done. We spend so much time overthinking, overanalyzing, judging, and stuck in the past that our best moments and opportunities sometimes fade in the bustle of our immediate concerns. We spread ourselves thin concentrating on mistakes, only to realize too late that this frustration was only a result of our inability to be happy and grow from the past.

Our minds progress from thought to thought like an assembly line. We start with something basic, like a mechanical part, that doesn't hold great meaning on its own. Once we put more into it, however, it can amount to something of much greater value, like a car. Likewise, our thoughts evolve into big ideas, opinions, and feelings. If you let a small negative thought evolve into something much greater, you may find yourself consumed by bad thought patterns rooted in an imaginary problem. Don't let the fear of missing your goals get in the way of your plan for success. Understand your mental tendencies and resist this downhill slope.

If you are afraid of failing, receiving poor recognition for your efforts, or just of putting yourself out there, recognize that you would be more exceptional for trying than for hosting ideas that never see the light of day. Exchange your thoughts of *One day* for the confidence that today is day one. You will become so many different figures in your own life. There is so much to achieve, seek, and conquer, and it's all up for grabs. Being happy is one of the best choices you can make every day. Decide to live your best and fullest life, but be honest with yourself. Ask yourself:

> Am I ready to commit to becoming the strongest me?

Do I have a major goal and a plan to execute
it?

_____

If your answer to both questions is yes, that's
amazing. Get started today. If either answer is no,
not yet, or you don't know where to start, then start
here and now. Live for yourself, free of comparison.
Live intentionally, and live by your own standards of
excellence and success.

Be the judge of your life, and understand that
no one has traveled your unique path, so no one is
entitled to judge your decisions, dreams, or methods.
Focus on your come up and your success story. Do it
for you and because you want to. That's the key to a
fulfilling life: living for yourself and not because of
someone else.

See your life for what it is, not for what it
should be. We often make excuses and find reasons
for the way things are. But sometimes life is just the
way it is. Don't think that life is against you; just live
in reality, not in a utopia and not in sufferance.

Realistically, are you over- or under-
compensating for the reasons you aren't achieving
your goals? Be honest with yourself and reflect:

What can I let go of today that's holding me back?

_____

Where does my commitment need to be strengthened?

_____

What excites me the most about my life?

_____

Am I ready to reboot my life and become the most fierce and most phenomenal version of myself that I can be?

_____

What am I waiting for?

_____

Look at the concept of life objectively, not personally. Use the tools and resources around you to change the trajectory of your life for the better. It's common to overlook the fact that the small decisions we make in each moment are the reasons behind the biggest changes and differences in our lives. The small actions we take today are what transform our dreams into reality. Take things one at a time. Choosing to be present in your life will make your successes that much more rewarding because as you go through the motions of true dedication, focus, and attentiveness you will realize that conquering your goals is nothing short of hard work.

Allow yourself to think and achieve broadly. Ordinary people will expect you to stop due to the limitations they assume about life: *You're not qualified, It's too hard, Your idea won't work*. If you can see it in your mind, you can achieve it in the world. Don't allow yourself, and most definitely don't allow others, to put restrictions on your life. If you're not qualified, get qualified or prove that you already have the skills. If something's too hard, do it anyway. If people assume your idea won't work, demonstrate that it will. Own the confidence in your dreams and aspirations. Sometimes you have to show others your promises rather than tell them.

To grow into the most powerful version of yourself, you must stop looking outside for validation, permission, and answers. Everything you've ever needed to achieve and all that you are destined to conquer has always been within you.

Start with yourself. Deep down, you know

what you want, who you aspire to be, and all that you long to achieve. You might be intimidated by the scope of where your ideas reach and how powerful they are. That's good: Your ideas should be big and bold. Bring them to life.

You are important and capable. Tone your craft and your ideas, and take your time. But when the time is right, I hope you will hold nothing back. If you've ever wondered what your purpose was, you would never find it on Google, in a classroom, or in someone else. Ideas can be sparked by various platforms, but your meaning lies within you. When it is blended with passion, drive, and focus, your purpose will be enhanced.

Your purpose lives within you. It's why you wake up, why you get up, why you think how you think, and why you live your life the way you do each day. Discovering your purpose and nurturing it is just a matter of eliminating the distractions from your progress.

Most people never start because they're simply afraid to begin. But there's no skipping your struggle. Train your mind to see your struggle as the jump-start to your success. Challenges always seem harder before you begin. Once you get through them, you are made better for what's to come. Whatever you have to overcome will make you stronger and mightier. You'll start seeing progress when you stop selling yourself short and quitting when things get tough. You must come to terms with your passion and decide you want it more than you fear it.

I find this part exciting—the moment when you realize that something inside of you is speeding up your heart. The moment that makes your eyes open wide and makes you think *Aha* and say *Yes, this is it*. The part that keeps you up thinking late at night and wakes you up early, revitalized and ready to work. This is the making of what will set you apart and satisfy your yearning for who you were always destined to become.

Risks lead to growth. If you miss, you'll learn that you need to try harder, approach it differently, work smarter, or figure out an alternative. If you win, you elevate, refine yourself, and discover room for new ventures.

Doors open as a result of your achievements. When you grow, you inch toward becoming your best. All of your successes are added to your personal portfolio—the mall of your accomplishments. Ultimately, these strides contribute to your happiness. New information, good or bad, will demand a shift in your perception, and this shift will ignite growth. Your elevation can only make you better.

◆◆◆

In the past, a woman was expected to yield at the crossroads of who she could become and who she was. Run towards who you can become. Do not stop. Become her. Obtain a forward-thinking, growth mindset. Your abilities can always be developed and matured. Capitalize on your brilliance and uniqueness.

There are unlocked abilities, thoughts, and ideas within you. Pursue them. Take your life day by day. The distance you have to go before your dreams are reality can be dispiriting. Still, look ahead but from the perspective that the journey is what will make for your beautiful success story. Your journey is the *only* way to make this success story, and you will get through it all.

Let your moral compass guide you. Reject what society tells you about yourself. Society doesn't know you, but you can make yourself known. Well-intentioned or not, society has a way of boxing you in. Family members, professionals, teachers, and even strangers pick paths for you sometimes before you can even refuse them. This is not your destiny. Be original, be an outlier, be purposeful.

As you mature, it will become clearer what is best for you, but only you will be able to determine that. Only you can determine the perfect path for your own life. Only you have to live and operate in your body, so stay in control. Recapture your life, and navigate on your own terms. Find your equipoise.

Every day, we are blessed with another chance. We are granted another opportunity to seek success, to be greater than we were, to chase our dreams, and to fulfill ourselves.

Success and an incredible life are no accidents. You have to live them on purpose. You must be intentional. You are worthy of life's biggest blessings. I believe that happiness is among the highest levels of success. Free yourself from the emotional chains and burdens of unworthy individuals. Put yourself first, and you'll soon see yourself in a totally different space mentally, spiritually, and physically through elevated confidence, augmented peace, and new opportunities.

Strong women are incredible and are essential to all aspects of the world and life. We are competitive, independent, disciplined, passionate, and reliable, all while preserving an innate kindness and affection for others and ourselves. We make the human experience better for all.

Make simple yet personal contributions to the world and to yourself by reminding yourself of four things daily:

1. **Be thankful for another day.** Be grateful that your eyes are open, your heart is pumping, and your mind is working. Even on your worst days, you are bountifully blessed because you woke up today to be great and live purposefully.

2. **Work on your goals.** Progress yields results. Your dreams will come to life and this will happen only through your initiatives and work.

3. **Be kind to and love others.** Uplift, encourage, compliment, laugh, and smile. Living in the moment reveals to us that our human lives are not eternal, and we should embrace one another everyday while we can.

4. **Be kind to and love yourself.** Speak goodness to yourself, live lightly, and work laboriously on improving who you are daily. This book is your reminder that you are not done with yourself. You are an eternal project.

That last part is the most important. Self-love is the best and the most important love there is. All growth, development, and evolution come from it. Understand your worth, understand why you are a gift, and recognize your strengths. Unlock your fullest potential from within. Explore yourself in search of the fullest life you can possibly live, and continue to search—not for someone else, but for your passion, your purpose, your plans, and your potential.

Master your destiny. Design the strongest, most fierce version of yourself today. Evolve into your greatest self, seek to understand, and be in tune with why your mind thinks what it does, what your body needs, and how to nourish your soul. Achieve the healthiest equilibrium of loving others and loving yourself. Life is changing every single day. Make sure the changes are increasingly positive.

I see the journey of life a lot like the way I anticipate the first day of spring. Despite the possibility of gray skies, chilly weather, and a few more weeks with my peacoat, I think about the brighter, fuller, happier days that will come. I yearn to feel the sun's rays illuminating and penetrating my skin. I never cease to admire the flowering dogwood trees that line the roads. I am interminably wonderstruck by daylight lasting past six o'clock in the middle of April. And I think I will eternally align the season's transformation with my own.

Use today to choose yourself. Use today to reflect, advance, and emerge as the best version of yourself that can exist. You are right on time in your life. Despite all the hiccups you've had along the way and the breaks you've taken on your path, all that matters is that you weathered the storm and you've arrived here, today. Your life is your garden, your promises are the seeds, and as beautiful as the first flower of spring is, I truly hope you let it bloom.

LIVE INTENTIONALLY

How have you prioritized yourself today?

_____

_____

_____

In what areas of your life do you feel most
confident?

_____

_____

_____

What is currently your number-one goal?

_____

_____

_____

What is your plan to execute it?

_____

_____

_____

THE QUINT*ESSENTIAL* CHECKLIST

Refer to this checklist daily to remind yourself of the many simple yet *essential* ways you can progress towards fulfilling yourself everyday.

Fulfill

- [ ] Stick with my goals
- [ ] Push myself to do my personal best
- [ ] Congratulate myself on my efforts, progressions, and wins
- [ ] Prioritize myself
- [ ] Choose to be happy

Understand

- [ ] Speak and think positively
- [ ] Practice self-care
- [ ] Cater to my body's needs
- [ ] Acknowledge and understand my thought processes
- [ ] Engage in something I want/like to do, not have to do

Balance

- [ ] Ensure that the energy and company around me is positive
- [ ] Appreciate my blessings
- [ ] Live in the present
- [ ] Love and uplift others
- [ ] Love and uplift myself

APPENDIX

Recap of In-Chapter Reflections
Chapter 1

⁜ Do I minimize who I am to accommodate others?

⁜ Do I set a higher priority on spending time with others than on spending time with myself?

⁜ Do I feel mentally stimulated by the people I surround myself with?

⁜ There are twenty-four hours in a day. How much of that time do I devote to my personal, physical, and mental health?

⁜ How deeply do I understand my motives, thoughts, and emotions?

⁜ Am I capable of admitting when I need help?

⁜ How confident am I in myself and in my future?

+ What goals have I set for the next year, and what accomplishments have I achieved recently?

+ How substantially do I prioritize myself in my life?

APPENDIX

Recap of In-Chapter Reflections
Chapter 2

- How does who I follow contribute to my life?

- Do the posts I see change my mood?

- Do they improve my mood?

- Am I comparing myself?

- Is this affecting my mental health?

- What is something that people come to me for?

- What's one area in my life that I have a good handle on?

+ How have I developed my _____ (*a strength that you inhibit*), and how has that improved who I am, all around?

+ What sets me apart from the rest?

+ What tendencies do I have when I feel unconfident? (*Minimized opinions or comments, stuttering, increased heart rate?*)

+ How can I prevent this or control these habits?

+ What triggers me to feel unconfident?

+ How can I counter my response and overcome this?

+ Does my negative self-talk reflect what I assume others think of me?

+ Do I feel a certain way because **once**, in the past, things didn't work out as I planned?

+ Why am I dismissing my strengths and potential, despite the fact that I am amazing?

+ What is the vision I have of my present self?

+ In what ways am I in control of my life?

How can I reframe my life so that I'm in charge of me?

APPENDIX

Recap of In-Chapter Reflections
Chapter 3

- If you're in pain, what brought you comfort today? List something small or large.

- How will tomorrow be better?

- Do I understand my emotions?

- Do I speak positively to myself?

- Do I allow past frustrations to affect my thoughts and feelings even after I'm physically removed from the situation?

- How can I actively refuse this response and instead maintain peace in these situations?

- How many hours of sleep did I get last night? Is this ideal? If not, how many hours will I strive for?

- What outlets or activities do I enjoy that allow me to get out of my own head?

- What are my favorite ways to decompress at the end of the day?

- How do I practice self-care?

- What practices can I perform to get in tune with my soul?

- What values do I hold dearly?

- When was the last time I reflected on my life and who I am?

- How can I actively make time for this?

APPENDIX

Recap of In-Chapter Reflections
Chapter 4

- What standards do I hold for my partner?

- What standards do I hold for myself?

- How often do I listen to my gut?

- Do I consider both my logical thinking and my intuition when making a decision?

- What are three things that have made me happy this month?

- What are three things that have made me happy this week?

- What are three things that have made me happy today?

- What am I most grateful for?

- What is my favorite part about spending time with myself?

- Do I embrace periods of solitude?

- Do I embrace my life regardless of my relationship status?

- How do I balance individuality in togetherness?

- What benefits come with partnership?

- What are my favorite ways to express love?

- How do I slow myself down and return to the present?

APPENDIX

Recap of In-Chapter Reflections
Chapter 5

- Am I ready to commit to becoming the strongest me?

- Do I have a major goal and a plan to execute it?

- What can I let go of today that's holding me back?

- Where does my commitment need to be strengthened?

- What excites me most about my life?

- Am I ready to reboot my life and become the most fierce and most phenomenal version of myself that I can be?

- What am I waiting for?

NOTES FOR SELF-REFLECTION

NOTES FOR SELF-REFLECTION

NOTES FOR SELF-REFLECTION

NOTES FOR SELF-REFLECTION

NOTES

Chapter 1: Take Two
Peers, Sarah. "Statistics on Women in Engineering." Women's Engineering Society, 2018.

Chapter 2: Resurgence
Kierkegaard, Soren. Kierkegaard's Journals and Notebooks, Volume 4: Journals NB-NB5. 1843.

ABOUT THE AUTHOR

Ariel Simmonds was born on the Upper East Side of Manhattan in New York. She was raised in New Jersey where she attended both public and private schools. She is an honors graduate from the Bloustein School of Planning and Public Policy and from the Douglass Residential College for women at Rutgers, The State University of New Jersey.

With a bachelors of science in public policy and a minor in women's and gender studies, she has compiled her knowledge of women, culture, and society with her conventional millennial experience and wisdom stemming from emotional intelligence and personal growth in pursuit of her innate responsibility to fight the good fight for women's success, equality, and empowerment.

ACKNOWLEDGEMENTS

This book would not have been possible without the help of all the special individuals in my life, including my readers. Thank you for reading and for yearning for more.

To my parents:
Thank you for paving a path that refuses complacency and for always encouraging change, development, and improvement. You are both so creative, professional, progressive, and loving. Thank you for pouring all of who you are into who I have become.

To Karle:
Thank you for believing that I was capable of accomplishing such a large and important project. You helped me turn an idea into a dream and a dream into one of the biggest milestones of my life. Thank you for your endless support, ideas, contributions, and love. I love you.

ACKNOWLEDGEMENTS

To Sheryl:
Thank you for choosing to be a part of my life. I remember you every day. Your positivity surges through my veins, and I strive to be as amazing, inspirational, considerate, and kind as you were. The world needs more people like you. I love you so much. I hope you are proud of me.

To my brothers:
The three of us are all very different. I thank you and love you both for the roles you've played in my life. I hope this book is not only something that you enjoy but something that your future families and your friends will love and hold onto dearly as well.

ACKNOWLEDGEMENTS

To my contributors:
Greg, Ira, Auntie Sonia, everyone I promised to
leave nameless during the interviews that I
conducted to gather perspectives for this book, and
everyone who encouraged me and supported me
throughout this journey, I cannot thank you enough.
Your creativity, attention to detail, insight, and
support are all gifts beyond a price. You are
quint*essential*. You have made me and this book
better, and I thank you for that.

To my extended family, the Skerritt's and the
Simmonds':
You have all, as individuals, played pivotal roles in
who I have become. You are all wise and successful
in your own rights. You've all inspired me to
become the greatest version of myself, and you all
remind me that there is always more to achieve. Our
laughter, our love, and our tight support for one
another is something most people don't have, and I'll
never overlook that. Thank you all for being a part of
my life.

ACKNOWLEDGEMENTS

To my friends:
In your less vibrant moments, thank you for trusting me and for feeling safe enough to confide in me for advice. It was through those moments that I knew I had answers that could help others. I'm not perfect, and I don't have life figured out entirely, but I don't take it for granted that you have looked to me as an outlet in your lives. Thank you for making me laugh, making me grow, making me wonder, and making me wiser. May we always stick together and help each other advance.

To my teachers, mentors, and supervisors:
In the moment, we don't always acknowledge the role that people like you play in shaping our lives. Thank you for guiding me, teaching me, and even going a little too far. These were the moments that taught me the most. Thank you for your contributions.